BY MADELINE DEFREES

MAGPIE ON THE GALLOWS

MAGPIE ON THE GALLOWS

MADELINE DEFREES

COPPER CANYON PRESS

1982

Acknowledgments

Grateful acknowledgement is made to the editors of the following publications, in which some of these poems appeared in these, or slightly altered, forms: *Agni Review, American Poetry Review, Amherst Review, Chariton Review, Columbia, Concerning Poetry, CutBank, GiltEdge, Graham House Review, The International Portland Review, Iowa Review, Massachusetts Review, Missouri Review, New American Review, Ploughshares, Poetry Northwest, Quarterly West, Scratchgravel Hills, Sunbury, Willow Springs* and *Yankee.*

"Boatsong for Karen" first appeared in a portfolio of poems for the Genoa-New York Poetry Symposium, Poetry and Interpretation, April 21-25, 1980.

The following poems also appeared in a chapbook, *Imaginary Ancestors,* published by CutBank/SmokeRoot Press, Missoula, Montana, 1978: "Honesty," "The Bishops Bring Tablets of Stone," "Burning Questions," "Grandmother Grant," "On My Father's Side," "The Widow," "Gerard Majella," "Gilbert of Sempringham," "Emily Dickinson and Gerard Manley Hopkins," and "The Woman with Fabled Hair."

These poems first appeared in *Woman Poet—The West,* Reno: Regional Editions, Women-in-Literature, Inc., 1980: "Slow-Motion Elegy for Kathy King," "Keeping Up with the Signs," "Standing By on the Third Day," and "Gold Ring Triad."

"Census of Animal Bodies; Driving Home" first appeared in *Roadkills: A Collection of Prose and Poetry,* Easthampton, Mass.: Chelonidae Press, 1981.

The author would like to thank the John Simon Guggenheim Foundation for a Fellowship which assisted in completing this collection.

Copper Canyon acknowledges the support of Centrum and the National Endowment for the Arts.

Copper Canyon Press
P.O. Box 271
Port Townsend, WA 98368

FOR MICHELE, TESS AND TERRI:

Changed life, not taken; or taken, kept—
bold word, transcending sunlight and the probing root
that cracks the footstone where our Sisters lie.

Table of Contents

I. BEETLE LIGHT

II. IMAGINARY ANCESTORS

III. SEVERAL LIVES

I
BEETLE
LIGHT

Delirium—diverts the Wretch
For Whom the Scaffold neighs—
                    —Emily Dickinson

"If our words mean anything," he said,
"they mean that death is for us, not
only a private act, but a public event."

An artist always carries death with him,
like a good priest his breviary.
                    —Heinrich Böll

Census of Animal Bodies: Driving Home

My headlights raise them up: a dash
of blood, small gullets white, paws treading air.
No mercy for that twist of fur, the rush of travelers
streaming home, where these four-footed
kind, perhaps, were beamed
before some engine
gunned them down.

                    Riding the brake, I mount them
in the brain: splayed frog, black as the folded
cat I swerve to miss
although the spring is gone from both. Rabbit,
wild in my path—and spared. The hard
triumphal arch of chipmunk in mid-air, framing
the fixed eye, the old fear. Mud turtle,
one foot lifted
at the center line.

                    Last night's maggots
magnified four thousand times,
cleaning up after the highway crews. Sparrows
kamikaze dive
too near my windshield. Repeated swoop of magpie,
crow and hawk. Bad news
in the barrow pit where stiff birds
sing from the other side
come over. Along the river, look to the yellow

                                streak
ahead. Divided Highway. A tail that could have been
a brush—white stripe on black across
the middle of the road, not flush with the other.
I do not pass. Alive still
I plant my stone on wet lines,
crude beside these warnings: *You will
smell this death for miles.*

Plum Rain

Thick fall of plums struck my head
grazing the shoulder, stood on the ladder
beside me shaking the tree. Shower of plums
and yellow leaves, fall of the visible.
In the kingdom of thud, globes plummet to black
nets on willed ground. The irregular halo of birds
fled from the bough's grape bracelet
crowns the figure of woman: wrist   ankle   amethyst
snare.

A stampede to frost-covered ground, the damson
cascade stains the palm. When I wrestled
stem and cheek for the plum of early summer, rich
in its own shade clinging, meat hard as carved walnut
locked on its own flavor.

Jack in the nursery
poking his famous thumb in the pie
meant to ornament his singular goodness. Long after
pail and wheelbarrow give over the nest
I wear purple eggs in plumtwig hair, singing
harvest to the winecellar under the load.

Slow-Motion Elegy for Kathy King

I roll the pebble of this word on my tongue, feel
the sting, the hard
salt taste of it. They never get it straight.
No way to splice the reel of wreck
and exile, the silent
film. You have passed on
to life in that cloudy home, leaving your friends
weighed down, shortening days
without you.

        Into the world, into the cloister
and out before me: whatever the future held
you held it first. Two sides of an old oak door
we traded supervision during lunch
and startled high school seniors with our French.
That year the enemy who struck you down
enlarged your heart. How soon these summer
reruns make me sad.

        Twelve months in bed and you were
back mountain-climbing stairs.
To think I envied you the sound track
fading out, the rest.
A walk-on strangler found the fire escape and broke
your dormitory sleep.
You said it was a shortcut
to a private room, the violence you dreamed
locked in by a double door.

        I saw it mirrored there.
Left behind, trying to name this
anger, this more-than-morning sickness, I interrogate
the tide. When you were mugged
police said, Do you still believe in civil rights?
A terrible neighborhood: They didn't ask you twice.
I watch you moving in to stay. Your brave words

skipping stones farther out than mine. Now they are
going down, coral and skull to lime.

                              If I could
match that other orator, the sea, I'd rage
out of bounds, beat the rock
you threatened. Lashed to the mast but never tied
to the script. No child
wearing a halo
ladles the ocean into this hole at my feet. A tourist
stalking elegant cuisine
appears to me. How easily the mind snaps
shut on itself, a razor clam.

                        How shall I know
the changing woman I am: the hermit crab scrawling
a private code. Dolphin, smart and playful,
towing a man-sized brain. The killer whale spouting
news of deep water. Nothing's
the right matter. These waves break over me
and break again.

Framing the Outdoors

When the mind rides at anchor I follow
that grieving woman
down broad steps leading to placid water,
the tiered concrete

                taking her slowly in.
Her scarf reddens the swan's throat, illusory
trees huddle around her figure.
The cupola dips white

                    where roofs converge
in welcome. The bronze spire dives
all the way to the weathervane, to the pool's
remembered floor. A black horse

                        gallops north
into the veined iris. The rooster turns and
turns into floating dark. The eye of the lake
turns everything back, opaque day

                    reversed
in black water. Neon swerves to describe a door,
calling the torn bird down, through the louvered
dome of afternoon. Only the unruffled swan

                            rides
home to the dim, limitless city, architecture
of breast and neck
prolonged for this ponderous dying.

From the Clerestorey

The monk who fasted all morning dips his bread
in a little water at noon.
"While it soaks I'll read a few verses
of Holy Writ." Soon he is lost
in comtemplation, the desert slowly receding
towards sundown, made bright by the vision
of water.

       He cannot know whose hands will lower
this coffin of refusals: what patch,
niche, plot, beyond doubt, welcome the traveller
home. In earshot the mirror-report of feet
slaps to a stop on flagstone.
Shot bolt, and a bar of sunlight widens
into a corridor.

       The shaft falls on the glow
of his tonsured pate,
curves light to a rim that may be a halo.
In the corner, desert bread
expands to the gradual side of the bowl, a bell
calls everyone to Matins.

       Far off, he hears
the brotherly chant of those choiring voices.

Hanging the Pictures

Every day I hang a different picture. They are
mostly the same—Vermeer's girl
in blue turban—a woman, clothed or not,
looks from the matte into distance, the first time
knowing her name.

What holds together or binds,
syllables roll on the tongue. No matter
how late, how ordinary or not, the given
covers the rapt body, wine-colored dress—Dolce—
lowered into light.

Figures assume a shape she has
always practised, cat and cricket shut out
where sleep cannot touch them. The other night,
good luck in the house, I killed a cricket, the second
one got away.

The left-handed woman whose thought
is awash on my wall, and the tree that is always a woman
held in the storm's wake, a sky
not her own and larger: they are the same white
body of the charcoal nude who brings back the strait

and the water's precision, gradually louder, lapping
ashore. I drive two nails into wood to hang her.
On the floor Modigliani's red-haired woman
falls forward into the room's frame and a black
leap I recognize but cannot stop from singing.

The day you were leaving

the lock stuck on the attic door,
a bolt slipped into gear
for the last act, the forked dark
under the rafters
closed on itself. I took to my bed,
ice pack heavy on lids
as shells driven through holes in the skull
or weight slung from crossed winter limbs.
Someone who put on
my old voice from a drained throat
said lines you wanted to hear.
Smoke collapsed around hair that clung
to the brush. Ash drifted sill
and floor from trays
left to please empty themselves, the days
and the night you were leaving.

The House on Broadway

The ice jam under Smitty's Pancake House means
business. All day firemen
pole their boats upstream towards Agnes Morgan
knitting on the front porch roof
her muffler bargains with cold airs
twenty-four long winters
in the downstairs flat.

In the street blocks float by her, steady
as the body of a man.
Three customers in underwear below the bridge
watch the backhoe grapple with dead trunks and sludge
to force an opening. Lines tied to shore
secure shorelines for the utility man.
It's a mean business.

Walker said the water rose very fast.
Imagine fisheyes
caught in great chunks when the stream loosened
and the dinghy fishtailed forward.
Arms of the man
machine with pikes and hooks, the war of water
on the banks, abandoned women.

That jam took care of itself, the operator said.

Beetle Light

for Daniel Hillen

Hornets collect on the side of the sun.
Windows I cannot open
magnify their frames. Whatever beam insinuates
itself in squares I cut across
fades the color underfoot and turns my aim
deadly. Sitting by your shade, dreaming
stained blue light, I weigh New England
dark against my palm and peer
through bottle green, milky accumulations
of the night.

        Overhead, black light in the socket,
broken neck of bulb, the filament
connected like a nerve. Someone has tried to get rid
of the irremovable shade, a welder's gun
turned against a coffee tin. Nailed to the rude
beam, nothing will bring it down. I return to antique
brass, your art and mine, to kerosene,
candlelight, flash of battery and morning rays,
small at first, burning away
the fog.

        Bodies accumulate. Small flies repelled
by cold. Dusky millers
stupefied in glare. You watched them cross your palm
and kept their slight iridescence
mounted in the brain, wings free as forms your glass
borrows. I prefer bugs at a distance: in plates,
in print, because I am less violent behind a screen.
Brittanica's hornet is sheer catharsis, a social
wasp, strikingly colored. The sting again.
Armed with a fly swatter, I watch one lift off the page,

begin to sing, the comb without the honey in the attic.
I darken towards the unexpected
spring. My plain-cooking landlady favors self-reliant
poets. They moon and thrive, trouble-free
tenants of the upper air. When I complain she mocks
the exterminator. Very soon they will die.

Dry Falls

No water drops over the lashed edge
to ease the dry socket. The pale-
veined year dies slower
than a nerve, will not congeal. Each
morning lid thickens a hairbreadth,
locks go limp as houseplants,
tenants disappear indoors. Through film
curtains they watch the ice cap
creep down where a thin creek
turns on itself and goes still. In thick
haze their eyes frost over
with cowled figures who cannot tell
fountains from trees. Light
falling from poles. Day's polite thaw
stiffens towards night under the bridge
where the circling will not let go:
that pull to the dark center. Map lines
converge.

       The doctor, dependable
friend, guides the blades of his skis
to a soft landing a thousand miles
from Thompson Falls, and the tow rope
slips through the warp of my hand.

Standing by on the Third Day

Coming late to your bed in sleet-ridden
halflight, the moon
lay on her back in the western sky.
Mountains stood in a ring at the cloud-
covered head, their weight
slung over my waist like a sleeper's leg.

In the flare of twin-engines, I count my age
in geologic time. I am too young
to leave. Plunged in the ship's wake
this comet opens a crater underwater
deep as the one inside. Bad weather in Denver,
the fallen stars. I have to get out while I can.

You hid the scar I held like wounded
feet to my lips. Exploring caves,
you rounded the last
boulder, laid hands on the slow
rise of my body, giving me back a life
that had been let down.

The drone of circling aircraft takes us home
to the island. Staid rhythms prevail
in northerly wind. It crosses my mind how
under the worn serge of a habit another code must
be broken. Whatever vows we speak
will break over our heads in fire or beat the cove
that gave us momentary shelter:

                          We have only
this night and the one behind it.

Birthday Poem

When the Hellgate wind unwinds down the canyon
and I wade in my tallest boots
one drift at a time; when that white devil
spins back mean in my teeth, the whole
jaw aching, I sometimes enter
the largest pyramid of all
and fail to emerge from the other side.

Some days that soft intruder climbs the window
ledge I watch, snowbound
at home. His face lights a clear moment, goes out
in chaff. My pulse slows down,
guides the writing hand. I sit with the lights off
tracing hard angles on the pane, sheer fall and rise
of the brain's oscillograph.

                        Carnations arrive
from Wylie Street where danger's kept
insured. Blear wash of sun
in broken ground. I follow engraved wheels to food,
one tread at a time. A Pinto clanking chains
recalls the heavy end of a car,
nose down in the ditch. Pale weeds by the road
mime themselves before going out unwept.

By midnight, the engine overhauled, shipshape. Cold
settles down beside me when I crawl
between the sheets. Flowers in their own dark
flash under lids: white pink, white yellow,
white-violet-red. All of us drink deep that life-
replenishing powder. I sleep in my shroud sail
like a first-class martyr.

Recessional from the Cloister

This tower window, for instance, is not a prison
for maidens with floating hair, nor the bell
that inspires legend. We call the shower room
the Civic Center. Surely that tells you
something. In the small enamelled washbowl
tides of disinfectant ebb and eddy
the tower bell dividing the day
spilling the Angelus over the valley.

                          Saturday
forenoon, after the early prayers, doors propped
wide on ladder and broom, Dolorosa the Dutch Cleanser
nun, geared for battle in coverall apron,
glooms over the alien terrazzo. Takes her stand
wringing out the mophead. Lately retired
general of the war on germs, she's a five-
star veteran of defiant stalls—Dolorosa: Dolorosa
come to terms with a fibrillating heart.

Heir of the rite, I am her sterile first aide,
vigilant washer of hands. At ten I wouldn't eat
anything not from a sealed box, the time
fresh meat in my aunt's kitchen drew flies
and live turkeys—mean ones—gobbled in the front
yard. Except for Mother, I might have lived
happy in a bubble. Polished and scoured, tutored
by Dolorosa and my faintly murmuring heart.

                            Schooled
in another Academy, Matt Talbot planted an unwashed
foot on perfection's ladder, hoisted himself
never cleaning his nails. To each
his own, intones Dolorosa. In spite of onslaughts,
modernism, and making due

allowance for radical canons, cleanliness remains
next-door neighbor to the godly: Dolorosa dictates
the terms of a fibrillating heart.

                          Flirt a rag
over chrome, skate around the bathtub
ring. Campaigns against grime set Dolorosa off
grimly after dirt and her crippled heart
protesting. Face inside the coif
turns whiter than the basin for liturgical
dipping of hands. First, remove the headdress. Undo
the cape collar. Chaplain, swing open the doors
on the crooked little smile and the dirge
rehearsed for Dolorosa of the fibrillating heart.

Keeping Up with the Signs

Meadowlarks nesting March to August yield
to summer traffic in the dovetailed grass.
Three clear notes. Do Not Walk in Open Field.

I run the way my feet suggest. Upheld
by ringing turf and larkspur flash, I chase
meadowlarks nesting. March to August yield

sways heavy on the cornstalked land I flailed
to find the spot where larks come less and less.
Three clear notes do not walk. In open field,

runways the wind lays flat, fill up. Revealed
in the natural clutch called happiness:
meadowlarks' nesting march to August yield

in the tilt of wind, rainswell and the cold
mating ground, to bed with the dangerous
three. Clear notes do not walk in open field.

I leave five clues for the field guide whose wild
speculation turns the head. Shells express
meadowlarks' nesting march to august yield.
Three clear notes do not. Walk in open field.

Portofino

Why, on this wine-
drenched reef of wind
and palm, of wave
and pine, do I recall
black coat and tails,
white vest, the singing
past, and a finch
pressed flat as a leaf
turned gold in the fall?

Settling into the A-Frame

                              In this loft the red portiere
opens on sleep and the sleepwalker,
country of clay pigeons tossed in air, the wished-for
shuttle weaving through flat haze.
Behind the yellow door
light puts on gauze and bangles, arranges
limbs of an odalisque in storm windows.

                              Caterpillars
intent in far trees, wind themselves in clouds
of unknowing. The Wandering Jew screens a bare window,
rooms all angles and bars. To live at such a pitch
under the eaves, morning
turned away in a flutter of branches, the prospect
green as my early years on the other
side of the continent.

                              Doors breaking the still white:
slashes of color. Behind the jade
green water bends to my least command, takes the shape
of my body. Wound in the arms of everything
left in a sojourn among mountains, I view the body
of this day, this three-sided
dwelling on upright beams, the horizontal aim

that lifts me up and brings me down. The air fills
with nails, harsh drive of crows. The left-
armed cross outreaches its partner, two sides of a triangle
built of ceiling and shadow. This woman I walk through
on my own, never sure of the switch, inserts
a nail in the wall
outlet. I leave with my hands on fire.

The Register

All night I hear the one-way door sigh outward
into billboard glare. The ninth-floor
cul-de-sac left by the wrecker's ball, my new
apartment.

          Inside the known hotel, décor of watered
silk and fleur-de-lis, the French Provincial
red-and-white, mine for the night, no more. A weak
bulb wears a halo through the dark.

                      The street
divides below the skid of rubber burning. One branch
leads to a hill's last word, one into morning.
Flying in place, hung from its thirst, hummingbird
in the honey throat of a flower.

                Bless me,
Father, I have sins to spare and love
these relics of the hybrid years I spent afraid
to move. Chant of common life, field lilies, all
that labor, too cautious then to spin.
Not even Solomon would know these regal lily flowers,
translated fleur-de-lis my wall
provides, the glory flowers-*de-luce*, of light breaking
clean on the iris. I open
my eyes to the light.

             Bless me, Father,
under heavy sun and hoping
still to make your life my own. I cannot nullify
the work this body's done
nor call each act religion. Wherever one road
joins another, blind, I think of you
and conjure up the loss. When two roads, gaining
speed, speed up to intersect, I cross
myself and lay the body down, arms open for what comes
to pass. Father, I am signing in.

II
IMAGINARY
ANCESTORS

Not a ship of fools but a cargo of disembodied voices. We will take on hands, they said, and assume our faces. We will build you a personal history out of the spars and rigging saved from the wreck.

Honesty

Money doesn't grow on trees, my mother said,
leaving out the dollar plant
dried in the Goldmarks' garden. All winter long,
it was my pocketbook,
thin membrane laminating seeds
that could be counted. Everyone else said Money
or Honesty. Mother rode trolleys,
waited for the stage.

That was the year her face flattened. Towards the cement
plant, the mint stretched
to the river. Crushed, it smelled like a letter
from Grandma, the one we never met.
Silver-haired and always
sending candy, she was my secret redeemer.
My brother said she hated the pope, Peter's bark
worse than Eve's famous bite.

We're not made of money, Mother said, and Grandma
shipped crates of oranges
that grow largely in California. The Book of Knowledge
showed *Lunaria*, tall with a silvery spetum,
called it everlasting.
I wrote it all down, hidden in the chest
with my underwear. Summers at Rockaway, I collected
sand dollars.

   Moonwort, I said. Dipping my toes
in water I waited for incoming tide.

The Bishops Bring Tablets of Stones

Mother went to school in a cyclone cellar. She learned
not to fight long-haired cats,
not to interrupt or make noise, not to lie
or cry over nothing. Neighbor boys were bad. Mother
prayed and believed in bishops—martyred Valentine,
St. Nick. Bring me a doll, she wrote in a newspaper
clipping. In the postscript, Don't
bring me a redheaded doll.

                      All the stories had happy
endings. The barn wrapped in barbed wire
delivered to the next farm
earned a new cottage at the St. Louis Fair.
The paraplegic owner of the ax
hurled through an oak
took his show on the road to success, and Uncle Joe
looked away from the rattler in time.

                      For once the parental
P.S. meant something. Our teacher said, Your letter
is a picture of you, tidy or not. What's important
belongs in the body. Mother's tissue-wrapped
curls in the tin box held
red glints. Auburn, Mother said, combing the evidence.
The bishop who rode a mule called her
strawberry blond. By the time I came on the scene
it had turned grey.

Burning Questions

Three times a week Mother set fire to the orphanage,
watched it burn to the ground.
If we poked among cold ashes we learned
records were destroyed. She cried over what we might
find. When the sun reappeared
she wrote letters: Tell me the true facts. You must
be hiding something. She thought
U. S. Grant had left her a fortune, too extravagant
for an orphan. The letter came back.
She tore up the Poles. What do they know? she said
watching eyes in the mirror
that were clearly Irish. They've mixed up the notes.

My father worked a bank that went broke. She took
to remodelling his side of the house. Dad
couldn't escape the perfect picture
frame. She turned him French overnight, beat the Dutch
out of his name, dabbling in white-collar crime,
the capital flourished in the middle.
That was before the Idaho Panhandle. It was great
on the Payette Bench, Mother said, looking
magisterial. The Blackfeet came into Brother Gene's
store and you had to watch them like Indians.
On our floor her wishes were law. For a minute
I nearly forgot she was Mother.

Grandmother Grant

Not the rejected lies of the New York Foundling
home, not the adoptive widow of two names,
one of devious spelling,
not the dogtag pinned to the plaid dress
for the train ride to Missouri, but the surname
worn like a shoulder brand
on the skin of the natural mother,
Grandmother Grant.

When I went in my black robes through the hot
streets of the city, a young nun
pale as the star I followed
led to the desk of a three-faced guardian. One
face called me Sister to my face. One was
motherly: "O my dear, I can't risk the wrong
information." One, older than the order, nervous,
bit the sentence off
on a fragment of Irish history.

I couldn't get past the gate. I recognized
the road I was on
led to heaven or hell. Either was barred,
date too early for the name.
A Closed File. I should tell my mother to come.
Back home in Oregon, sixty-nine, wanting to know,
not wanting to know, she waited.
I crossed the continent angry, three thousand
miles of featureless plain.

Mother, now that you're gone, I'm the same,
swaddled no more in the habit.
Whatever it is that drives us—bad blood,
the face in the unlighted window,
I'm bound to get it straight. If he knocked her down
in the stinking hold of a ship and raped her,

if she followed him out of the church
into the oldest garden under moonstone limbs
of the sycamore, it's too late
to cover her tracks.

                Whoever she was, whatever ties,
here is my claim. I need to come into my own.

Ulysses S. Grant (1822-1885)

The Treasury voted nine to one against your ordinary
chin, though you cut mustache
and beard to sit for the profile photo. With Liberty,
that noble woman, your dreams of fame were half
dollars, the silver part
aristocrat like millionaires of Boston Common,
the homespun sage of almanacs, obverse
eagles and bells.

         More than the rest, Mother believed
blood tells but wouldn't say what. She
claimed you—with or beyond reason—saving the pencilled
Mary Grant pinned to the front of her faded plaid
like an heirloom. I read available
histories, imagined Army tanks of social disease
rolling down, a plague on my doorstep. Expected my mind
to go off, the slow tongue
fused by drink and vague neglect.

         Under the West Point
manners and epaulets, beat the timid heart of a store-
keeper. I joined your campaign against migraine,
kissed your clay feet warm, hung over
the bedpost, head split clean as rails of your honeymoon
cabin. In Mother's kodak, Dad stands in knee-length
coat, starched shirt and hat, one hand on a post,
stunned by the history he's come into.

         On the back
in Mother's cursive hand, a legend of relationship
to Julia Dent, Grant's First Lady.
It makes no sense without a double tie, adoptive
mother and real in league
to right some kinsman's wild throw. *Little pitchers
have big ears*, Mother says, and so

the story closes. I watch the smoke from a president's
quota—20 cigars a day—ticket

                                    to cancer of the throat
and memoirs written, dying. A family man to the end
he sold his life for wife and children. Even now
the overheard alarms. Mother died of a perfect heart
tracking invented lives through the land, the record
always partial. I look to her nine-years' grave
through a light sifting of snow, travel cold
as she lies without a coat of arms.

On My Father's Side

Off the coast of Council Bluffs, Great Grandfather's
ocean liner went down. Years before
he sailed into the plan of God
Mother was already waving. She knew his ship
would come in, another miracle. I studied
the map of my head, painted the hull
orange. The mainsail was blue
over musical water. Nobody understood
how I fell heir to
the size of his hands like my father's.

All night in my head going down, the sea-keen
of his wake. I wrote his lament in the book
covered with envelope linings.
No one in this family can carry a tune, Mother said,
and I carried it to the attic. Safe there,
I threw my rag doll
a life preserver in the flood of infallible
pronouncements. My father's father's father's voice
rolled like the sea
through my father's impossible speech.

Emily Dickinson and Gerard Manley Hopkins

My notebook shows they took a formal cruise,
floated past bridges in the morning light.
From cliffs of fall to mid-Atlantic blues
they traveled fifteen knots the day her White
Election fell to his Ignatian news
of still pastures and feel-of-primrose night.
I owe my life to that New England nun
and triple locks the musing lover sprung.

In Amherst Emily prepared to risk it:
she scrawled some verse on napkins, tucked the wild
game in a hamper, doubled a batch of biscuit
dough and stepped over her father's threshold
while the old man napped. Too timorous to ask it
—he may have dreamed her docile as a child—
Gerard approved, leaving his Company behind
for her improbable liquor, out of his mind.

The world they charged led soon to a famous wreck:
both saw it looming off the coast of Wales.
The demure velvet ribbon about her neck
was not a leash, and cautionary tales
rang true. Her cries rose with the waves on deck,
the lioness again, breasting the gales
that left her adamant to write the letter
granting each heart its stone for worse or better.

The first three drafts were bitter as dark beer.
The next seemed overlong; the fifth, too frantic.
She made a couplet timed to disappear
the instant one considered it pedantic
and for the stricken lute of the sonneteer
a veiled refrain of grief become romantic.
Not one would do. She'd have to write in bed.
He found her there and straightway lost his head.

She showed Gerard where he would find his own
pale eyes inside the velvet-tethered locket.
Poor Emily! How else could she have known
he carried Whitman in his greatcoat pocket?
It's best, I think, to leave the pair alone
until their dull dough sours on the captain's docket.
In any case there's no communion service
when this bread's gone and Emily is nervous.

How could she give him up to any storm
after the voyage shared—those breathless dashes—
a line all stress, or nearly so, a form
impervious as slag, set free of ashes.
Let others rest in harbor, safe and warm.
They found their comfort in the cold sea crashes
the black west sent to beat the soldier's cave:
that Roman collar carried to the grave,

laid like a wreath over the unmarked vault
where bones of ghostly lovers washed ashore
on her white beach. The sand ground from basalt
by wind and wave in the skull's unquiet roar
was soft-sift now, though powerless to halt
the glassed descent from ecstasy and more.
These brief affairs we label mid-Victorian,
seduce the timid soul of wit's historian.

"Gerard," Emily wrote, under a sky all sunset,
"It's over—like a tune—the sad Campaign
of Sting and Sweet—will never be the one let
soar—The Auctioneer of Parting—bid the rain
rehearse the dew." Her pen assailed the runlet
crossing the intimate sheet with a purple stain,
my Grandmother Dickinson, dyed in the clerical woof,
was warped for good. I am the living proof.

The Widow

There was a self-made widow far back in the trees,
wore black even in summer, black
to her unsung bridal. Knelt for the cross of ash
on lip and forehead, ash
sifting down to the covered breast, the ritual
giving of palm.

              That too eager martyrdom of wishes
sent before the blood, drained color
from the skin, leaving the breakable face
in the circular window. Truth
supported her, that ingrown toenail of the ordinary
saint walking on ground glass.

              Windows of unreal space,
her sanctuary opened on the widow's walk of miners:
everything learned by rote rejected, everything
but the guilt. See how the palm
droops towards wilting lids, eyes rolled
to her lord or her lord's envoy,

              halo conjured
from heavy air. Eyes cast modestly down,
the statuesque pose of eyes on a plate.
Never the clear gaze of the whole woman, always
sackcloth and lamentation,
the penitent's crown.

          Today October haze
crowns the mountain, leaves crack underfoot, shock
tilting the earth's crust. Black glasses I wear
peer through her eyes as I kick
the leaves aside and sing for the widow glass.
She falls at my feet breaking the cold surface,
ash floating on air the dust settles.

Galileo's Case Reopened

Lie still, son Galileo, while we crack
the seal, undo the nails and let the bronze
repeal of history correct your bones.
And what's three hundred years, the long trajec-
tories of moons, their lines criss-crossing like
a pinball game? Believe me, no one wins
without a slight distortion of the lens
changing the curve of inference and luck.

Timely as rockets bursting on the mind's
black earth, I plant the fleurs-de-lis of kings
over your grave to mark the faithful skull.
Inside the socket where the globe unwinds,
the shaken bell of every iris rings,
your brain flowers like a solar model.

Sister Maria Celeste, Galileo's Daughter, Writes to a Friend

Again I am at sea. If this be faith, it is not
the faith I bargained for
when I gave that troubled half-life over: the slow
sidereal day in trade for a guarantee
the drift persuades me to consider.

                                    This morning
lifting the shipboard cup from my lips into the hands
of my judges, the cheap wine cloying my tongue,
I see the rift clearly. Nothing—not words, the unlikely
notice of scholars, not the face
set towards a cruciform sun; least of all, the ritual
meant to distract us—eases this passage.

                                    I have
bargained everything away for the slow word, hard
as science, for an uncertain page
in the text of the future. Have taken in vain
the name of God's mother, coupled it with foreshortened
heaven. This is my home
voyage, too fast to be wasted in anger.

                                    Call me a vessel
come in from the peaks and valleys written in water.
Blot out my name. Moored to my own
tilted deck, I ride, I am riding
the battered hulk to the ocean floor.

What Makes or Breaks Them

Greatness was something in the bones: it meant
a kind of two-way stretch, sinner and saint
cut from the same bright cloth.
My namesake, Mary Magdalen, a case in point. These
were the better sort, and some
had gone the wrong way first as I had not.

From the convent cell where I fasted and prayed,
I studied the fine print of those loose
women who strayed door-to-door,
desert-to-desert, ending always in the right camp.
That was the mammoth risk, swung prehensile
over the Garden Wall.

I would have been less categorical, but in between
lay namby-pamby. I thought of the foreign
missions. Japan: sitting cross-legged
through ceremonial teas and formal addresses, barely
moving a muscle. Eating seaweed cookies, taste
of rotten fish.

              In South Africa, a slash from crotch
to gullet, not quite my dish, either. Vague
tales of babies delivered, learning to speak Sosuto,
the woman whose tumor weighed fifty pounds. I parried
the rain of stones on Christian heads
old men bought from the witch doctor.

                      Stuck on prim
rosepaths, I cultivated lilies and languors for all
they were worth. Sometimes a rift
in the wall, crack in the door, brought in the virile
drift of ocean, its salty crash. Carried away

by Margaret of Cortona's role, my head swam
to meet that model penitent.

                             Like hers, my days
and nights were spent in tears—without a checkered
heaven to make them credible. Mornings, chapel windows
wide, thermostat on 50, St. Mary of Egypt's desert
sizzled comfort. Her diet was inedible;
sunburn-cloak, less than modest. I admired
her walk on water, preferred

                                   alligator pears to lentils
at the farewell banquet, agreed the lion digging
her grave would be a smash on the dust jacket. Still,
I didn't have the nerve to back it up. The raves
rang false: early rapture, crocodile tears—most of all,
the late affair with Scripture—wouldn't wash.
The woman couldn't write or read.

Gerard Majella

Among ancestral saints Gerard Majella, tailor's
apprentice, took first place as well as second.
He could bilocate, served a bad-tempered
bishop. I wore his medal with the other
over my heart—Benedict,
saint of expectant mothers—under the black serge
cape, the reefs and shoals
of that halting voyage.

                     Gerard, they said you must not
attract notice, confined your wonders to such
as monks approved. I used to watch that careless
workman hang in clear air under the scaffold
before the cumbersome machinery
moved. Traitor to my land, I wanted words to come
to term more than I wanted God, clung to your blessing
hand, straddled the Great Divide,
cheered when you came from your ghostly father.

                             Stitching
unstitching hours in mid-air, the lines seemed a decade's
thought. They wound the dim passage in black
sleeves of Latin that sing to me yet.
You put the platform back under awkard feet
as I passed, rich, through the needle's eye, balance
restored and my mind
clear as the head in another planet,
eyes on the right ground.

Uncle Matt's Farm in Cherry Grove

The uncle not really an uncle, Mother's second-
fiddle makeshift dad, wore the same coat
to church and in the garden. His money wouldn't
stretch. He couldn't keep his head
above water, the uncle who had
to be taken away. Bill collectors trailed him
in the hospital: rec room, bathroom,

bed. Near a small water wheel on Uncle Matt's farm
I saw my first muskrat. I was eight. I stood
very still while the animal
went under water. Uncle Matt was better, but his coat
was too big. I was waiting for the cousin
not really a cousin I might marry later, who lived
in our house and played our piano.

                                           He brought
orchestras into our living room. When he was gone
I carried his postcards in my pocket, slept with them
under my pillow. Would he come home? Digging
shrubs in the hospital dirt, Uncle Matt found
himself. What he lost, I could lose.
That part made it hurt. It was everything.

The cards were beginning to crack and tear. I took
them and my books into the Cherry Grove
sun, tracking the print with a finger, following one
through the mud. I was glad and scared. I can still
bring back the pale whiskery scramble. The brown
coat, red where the frayed
light fell and the natural musk.

Eminent Victorians

Those years I hated them meant simply: I did not
love my chains. The click of rosary beads,
black olives around the waist,
made straight the way of strait-laced Sister Victoria
patrolling classroom aisles. Sometimes
as she bent to guide my pencil, I could surprise
a glimpse of neck under the shirtfront starch,
her guimpe's white circle
standing away from the body.

                                    I'd see myself
floating on billowy skirts, far from land's familiar.
Joining hands in the wrong order, I kept
my beads in vast pockets of unholy things: man-sized
linen handkerchiefs, scourge of envelope verses,
silk-lined purse for white veil pins
and thread. I learned to chant the Office of the Dead
in smooth Latin and detested those grotesque
small sinners Dickens sentimentalized.

                                    Remembered
Twist at ten: a cautionary orphan's story
I insisted suffering to the end
because I'd checked it out. In high school
I panned the thick fog of *Two Cities*:
Madame Defarge knitting away the French Revolution.
Would she send mittens and scarves like Grandma?
Recalling evidence of devotion,
I admitted Dickens' worldly wit
and made my first concession:

                                  Charles, we are all
in your debt, in your debtors' prison: writing
our lives, installments of a flight
pure as Jesus' walk on water. What matter
that the world is evil if our words contain it?
I watch the Seven Swords of Mary's sorrow

pierce Victoria's heart, spiked bouquet in a holy
frog, and marvel at the red
stain on the starched forehead, sign that Jesus
wants to share His crown.

        I plan to carry mine,
the veils and crosses, oil in my lamp: a ready Bride
on time for the Wedding Feast. Far from London's
seamy side, the one Dickens penetrated, I would
remain aloof, my legendary
life. I keep my eye on the models: cool as Jesus,
holy Bread in the tabernacle
I believed an icebox: Father, watch your priestly
hand—frostbite more dangerous than fire.

Gilbert of Sempringham

Plain Gilbert to me, who wore with a heavy veil
the luckless name let down by a bishop
on my shorn head: "Henceforth you will be known as . . .
Gilbert," the same given first
to a New York nun in an extant grave, who wrote
Our Nation's Builders, stacked
in the classroom cupboard.

The fifth grade clapped when I came. "Sister, did you
write this book?" their eyes bigger than the words
inside. I shook my head, refusing to claim
that honor, showed them the dictionary. The books
never wore out, their blocks
longer than chapters I learned to translate
a paragraph at a time.

Gilbert, my saint, if I had you my own, always
in the shadow of the great. "The real
Sister Gilbert was a saint, was she your aunt?"
Should I tell them I hated the murky lines? They quoted
her life of the foundress, room gone in the haze
of Mother Mary Rose, I tried
and the fifth grade was right.

O my English patron, believe I drew water from your
twelfth-century springs.
Only the Gilbertines survived, your order
of nuns, not the men
you gave them as masters: those and the crumbs
you scraped from refectory tables,
pledged to discourage waste.

I gave you the frugal ways of my imitative life.
How could I follow you, founder,

lost as I was with my foundling mother, starved
ghost of my convert father,
under a shroud at sixteen in all weathers, white
body lost in heat,
not even my name new-borne?

Ernst Barlach

Frost and Hunger. Your stolen title, the one thing left,
my Massachusetts weekly
check after taxes. It picks up a poet's
phrase for our time in Montana, a nice
security gone to hell.

                      Barlach said, For everything—
paradise, hell, one disguised as the other—there is
expressive form. He knew them all, last
of the realist sculptors. Cold fell. On Russian
steppes, knives turned
savage in the gut.

                 He set Slavic bone against the wind.
The laughing man laughed still, the sad
musician played. A solid peasant swirled his cape
before the swordsman wind. The rest is never
mind. In the end, a frieze of listeners
carved from missing hearts.

                     Intruder here, brash
westerner, footprints too recent,
thin on old New England rock, I pull on boots, my cupboard
bare, and look to Barlach for relief. "At bottom,
that's what we are—beggars, problem characters. In the Slav,
it shines out while others hide it."

                      The hidden
body of this waiting curves around waiting
forms, assumes the shape of a cup
extended. I beg sorrow to fill it up, flare like a bell,
ring the dissolution of the veil, hands
not knowing themselves
numb on the great bronze clapper.

The Woman with Fabled Hair

In the life to come I unravel and let down
the extravagant bolt of hair,
the braids of a saint caught in silk
all the days I remember. Cut free of the tin box
the future crown is always mine. Repeated
shocks of auburn, shades of my mother's
upswept hair when she ran away
with the man who would fade to my father.

I am waiting for him to come again, the simple
man in elaborate disguise, wearing his
bones like a prophet. When enough time has been
lost, her hair will fall to my shoulder.
Dense folds released from the veil, this past
woman's glory recovered
brings back the forgotten blend, lilac and
amber, cypress and plum.

The man will look into my eyes when I come
for the girl in the glass, the one to be
lifted down from the wall where she hangs
in the white dress, the too-short curls. "We have
plenty of time," taking the girl's right hand.
"We have from now on," stroking the nails
she tried to press down, kissing them. He won't mind
that her teeth are set far apart,

believing that passionate sign. *Don't be afraid,*
and the brain in its time carries her
over the doorstep, engraved words to a bride.
These forevers that keep
disappearing, bureau drawers of a life
that threatens to move us out. The body
meets the animal it ran from: dark bush
parted in the night, wet fur, the cave lighted
by the eyes of lynx, my own
dense longing.

III
SEVERAL
LIVES

Thin as a snail's track
on the mind's walk, the year
pulls back into its shell.
I skim the silver from the cracked
cement to spend it all
before winter closes down.

*   *   *

The Hammock's Motion lulls the Heads
So close on Paradise.
                    —Emily Dickinson

*   *   *

The other tongue
splits like a magpie's,
repeats any fire I teach it.

Scenes from the Great Round

1

Everywhere the moon traverses the night sky,
its light original and self-contained, a wheel
rolling on itself, the lunar seven
marking time. Houses of the moon are my house: I
am a vessel, an urn, I suckle everything
alive in the morning earth.
I wear an animal body.

A man arrives at the broken field, long planting-
stick in hand. He pierces
earth for the woman who holds
a calabash bowl to the femur. Handfuls of seed
open the realm, the first
seeds pressed in a child's fist, drop on plowed
ground the man moves on.

2

There is a desert on the moon, a crater with no water
where the least falling star falls on
the dreamer inspired only at night and by moonlight.
Tear out the heart for rain, and floods come.
All night driving the east shore, a lake of fire
gravid under the sun god. His disk parts the earth
turned to devour.

That man in the madhouse window squinting past sun
watches the cockeyed wind his head moves,
side to side, as the solar phallus turns
and returns to the womb. He is working back
to a crescent hammock, the Great Round of Wind-river
Mountain: Father Sky lying harmless
in his beginning on Mother Earth.

3

Maps chart the moonscape wrong. Where is the melon-
cactus the turquoise prince

stole from the Aztec madonna? And where are the singeu
butterflies tipped with obsidian?
The Corn Mother sings to her son in the husk: *what is
lost will return, what is torn
come back to the sickle.*

Phobias Incorporated

Father Giuliano, the drama instructor, fainted
every time he saw blood.
When a nun in the class, newly acquainted
with stagecraft,
fed a hand to the band saw, Giuliano was the one
who had to be treated. My mother
applauded the hero.

              At the first clap of thunder
she ran to the bureau for the rosary.
All through a stormy upbringing
under the kitchen sink after dark,
I repeated my lines. No wonder I link priest and parent,
twins in a Siamese startlement: Blood and Thunder,
Thunder and Blood. *Pray for us . . .*
at the hour of death.

             The real drama begins with
a thud—my sister—not claustrophobic, not
acrophobic, plunging from bed,
riding the nightmare bedrails. Her elevator shaft
endangered us all, marked women,
dumb waiters adrift on a sunken Titanic. Days,
I rode up and down, wherever the tenants were going
for fun, not pushing the panic button.
I was afraid of cats.

             It's a circular story
and that's where I leave it: the Siamese leap
sucking breath, old wives'
tales, the alley cats my sister brought home
sheltered from storm,
early death of a hero and always
the drawn blood informing
our several lives.

Gold Ring Triad

Cheerful as Martin of Tours dividing his cloak
with the beggar, my mother took that wide
souvenir from her finger to give me an equal share.
Her ragged sunflower face glowed with the brush
of her lover's hand, opened a space in air.
I ascended there, peered over fences of neighboring
yards, head half-turned to marauding
birds. Looked into the leashed
animal lives next door and a caucus of purple finches
campaigning against the cold. Already a chill
invades the old injury, the crooked knuckle stays

what's left of a double ring. With a narrower band, I
promised to marry no one, live for everyone
behind the high stone wall: it was a marriage in air,
a bond sealed until I could breathe
no longer in that zone high above the clouds. My head
quivered, a severed and perilous freight. To steady
the wealth of my own ground, I trespassed outside
the gate. Imagine a squirrel, sure-footed flagpole saint
sent into the closed fist of sky. Raffish
head, death's head, the ongoing neck: how exposed
the staff that keeps us vertical!

                              In this replicated
sun I praise everything that fuses clay
and fire: earth broken and tilled,
the usual harrowing
sign of division. And I remember pain, confined
by my portion, waiting in the hospital bed
for the disk to mend. My body
worn so thin the ring slipped from my right hand
and fell unnoticed. At home

I missed that relic of two lives
I could never find again.

                    And you, my sister, my friend,
knew my grieving, gave me back the dead
woman's share. I wore it on the left, hand of true
marriage, pledge sinister. Relic of unions
blessed though not made in heaven, my poor
lost mother, almost a child bride. In the first
luster of final vows I tried to appear older, rub initials
smooth. Her half, profane
from the start, bore none: no Jesus, Mary, Joseph
to pillow the dying head.

                    It was destined to take me
elsewhere. I wear that ring in bars, in bed, wherever
it fits, the right little finger
beside the opal that is not my stone: half-lost
ring of my dead mother
forgiven, ring of abandoned lives
knit into my own.

Sanding the Chairs

All the way down to clean wood where the grain
shows hickory and a chair
is what stands
after heavy lives settle in, and the housewives,
restless, sigh the spring
green, drying pale blue: dream Hollywood
in red enamel.

Every layer of paint, a country of wishes: the days
of townships lying in harbor
riding at anchor
follow the stars. And now, the women
lifted on domes of silence by musical chairs
glide over carpets to double duty
in the far bedroom.

The wrong feet on the rungs leave scars: they will
be gone when the fine dust settles.
Stripped down, legs tilted back in a bid
not to be tied to linoleum. Under the final coat,
bruise of buckle and clasp, the original
stain of the owner. For days
the curve of wood stays firm in the muscles.

For Paul Mariani Bringing Electric Broom
and Garden Produce

Daylight of roadside stands where pumpkins flare.
I'm a charged witch riding a hand-me-down
broom. So much to sweep out: old leaves, plaster
falling on the stair. I sweep dead popes
away, the hornet's nest, bomb scares, bad debts,
the world's tallest library and two swans
in collapse.

        Bless you, Paul, for the sack of garden
fare, broom on the wrong doorstep by the right
intent. The secretary who keeps things straight can't
miss the pope's blessing. What if I give her mine,
an even trade? Missing last week's J. F. Powers priest,
I hear Italian nuns are tearing off
the Holy Father's cassock buttons for relics. I know

how far I've strayed, crying over onions in old skins
as if they were new wine. I fill baskets
made for loaves, wrap tomatoes in a reliquary green,
assign the edible tuber a rubber nest. My oak table
drops both leaves, saluting acorn
squash, the gifts you brought,
acute relief from lentil soup I'm living on.

Morning. Slow turn past Herter Hall. The house
too clean. Shopping news and a check for three bucks
in the mailbox. I spend it all
five times. Four packs of filter cigarets. One-fifth
of a steam iron. Eight coffees, half with nickle
tips, not quite ten pounds of laundry. A double shot
to break the demon's luck.

        Walking 63, the old highway.
Dammed waters rush on rock near Pulpit Hill Road.
Truck wheeze and slackened engine

spare me once more. The sign for Sunderland. The bus stops here, not the one to Boston and the pope. Air thick as lentil soup, I'm hanging on, ready to stoke seven other devils calling home.

Aladdin Lamp

With luck and the slow hand of the lover
I polish the lamp
to its antique glow. Over the ring of incised
rectangles where the double wick climbs
I watch the girl
dreaming by firelight. She plucks
the burning pitch from coals, lifts it high as a torch
and escapes the small brass picket fence
into the next century.

Nothing goes on but the fire. Swirls of opaque
roses caught in a slender chimney.
Clear at the heart of the globe's
Victorian shade
she runs with leaping tongues, the steady beat
of the trackstar. Small legs
pumping down the block
into the street where skaters gathered and past
the great beetle light of the tropics.

Wood spits in the andiron grate. What do apple logs
know, too old to catch fire? The pale observer
shudders from the cold room
toward the milky dawn of Chicago. She says,
If I kicked over the lantern would the man up late
notice? Already the hillside moon
lifts a gnarled trunk in its tongs. Hurricane
sweep of barn and town. Sky
in the window blazes.

Sifting the Ashes

In some other life she traveled light.
—Leslie Ullman

Over Detroit the pilot spews choppy air into the mike,
our jet converting bird to burden
rolls the wind. I re-create the end, some
other life I wanted to travel
light. Not the snail, a spiralling
house on my back
leaving a silver trail of arrival.

                              It matters not,
the Fathers told, *whether a dove's held
in irons, linked gold or silk thread, so long as
she cannot fly.* Heavy roll in seaweed-tangled
spool of high cloud. Briefcase, lead underfoot. Coat
jammed in the rack. I want to strike a match,
watch my clothes blaze the eastern sky.

                                   Lifted,
bones turn phosphor. Every hair remembers how
fire split a two-by-four I couldn't cut, separated
bolt and nail from the third gate
that wouldn't shut, my house kept in kindling
all last winter. Carried out, ashes sing: buried
iron turns hydrangeas blue.

                         When engines fly apart
we'll cross trail we blazed on impact, mountain
nailed to your silhouette. This country's
never flat, marked by morning stars, ills the flesh
is heir to. High ground keeps your body warm,
my body under yours, the long wait over.

Picking Youngberries on Mr. Harvey's Land

Five hours by egg from noon, I am suing
my knees for support. The stretch
for the dark berry in a noose of morning glory
stains my hands, my jeans
bluer than heavenly pie through twined
thorn and I remember how the bear
hugged the woman
into another life in the park
for no reason.

Killer or lover, I would be sure of my clothes,
myself the blue intelligence
trapped in our capable bodies. Where
shall I leave these hands? Shall I give them
the studio rose, the cold
claws of dahlias shawled in blue air?
I am stained under glass, a choker
of vines like the green
housefall of the oakleaf croton.

Hands go on their own errands: white bells
in the pail, berries
fallen in trenches. The long canes
and my arms arching. Sun
lowered into a dark bucket, a faraway eye
drowned in the scene. Together
we lift the known
interchangeable sweets, our underground
dreams to a nave of leaded light.

Submarine Lamps: a Dialogue Overheard at the TM Poetry Conference

The water spider makes her home in a bell-
shaped chamber of silk,
anchored by threads to water weeds. This
is the meaning of invention.

To enter the bell, divers must pass through
the outer door, leaving the motor on idle
and close the door firmly after them.

                                    They
next swing wide the second door leading to
the main shaft, pass through that
and close the door after them.

Who could predict this forlorn diving bell
so far from the edge in the middle
of the Iowa corn?

                    The Pacific Ocean floor
moved rapidly and jumbled rocks appear
roughly handled. Bell divers were employed
to level the sea-bed. Clad
purely in woolen suits, neckties,
and watertight thigh
boots . . .

            Are you sure this is true on a deeper
level or are you working for the fishmongers
from Tibet?

                    When a diver settles into that
silky sea, the extra air
pressure to which he is subjected

is instantly
transmitted to the whole inside of his body.

Isn't this dangerous?

                  Most apparatus is fitted
with a telephone and submarine
lamps used largely. The diver is the soda-
water bottle, and his blood
the fluid in the bottle. So long as he stays under
that pressure, his blood
appears
to be unaltered.

             What if the battery's
too severe? Weather in the phone
sends a shock of corn through the mouthpiece
and the diver
wants out or through? He could suffer
the blackest death of all:
famine in a stew
of confusion, drought in a sea of trouble.

To expel the water, the spider disengages
the bubble until the water is replaced
entirely by air.

              No damage to lungs?
What about dust? Or rust?

This diving suit is independent of outside air
designed to withstand pressure. The diver
breathes air.

How soon can I go down?

Access to the working chamber is by ladder.
A helmet is provided with a non-return valve.

And if the pressure turns excessive, does it
make sense simply to wait
to float like the water spider?

                          You will grow
accustomed to living in tents, in air-
filled tents, creative coherence
lapping your bones under water.

Hanging the Doors

They are hanging new doors on the other side
of the mountains. Soon
I will pass through into snow
that halo of recovered friends.
On the island I enter
and leave by the window
a bed of leaves by the north stair
the cold ground floor of retirement living.

When the operator cuts off an ear the four-
party line goes dead. Door too wide
the carpenter takes orders from the owner
who gives the middleman her head
leaves the locksmith
to his own devices. A blade in the solid core
lets dark enter
a diamond sized to the eye.

Night fog rolls in windows where two red beacons
nail the other island to the channel.
I log eight hours under blankets to Lockhaven
drive through lanes of lovers shut
behind pearled gates, their waves
a water wheel turned slowly. Sleep
lifts the gleaming pail to light
a daytime flow of strangers.

To say I'm home I pass out keys to missing
lives. You store them in a vase
of spotted laurel. I am
tired of being wary. Please
be ready for the handshakes. No trapdoors
baited for a leg
no lung closed down from milling sleep
that breathing even.

The Second Move

That day in summer when I sold the bed I lay on,
paper, building a shaky monument
around me, proved too much. The kitchen
filled with the secondhand, my mother's death,
the overrated, and I neared the end
of grieving losses or their planned beginning
in a move I hadn't dreamed.

                    All night I ran
through light framed-in by the porch, the shade
of plum, to a place my car was missing:
left in a rented stall I would return to. The work
I willed to friends, beyond retrieving,
spilled from crates and whiskey boxes, makeshift
boundaries that told me what I'd had
in mind.

               I should have called Goodwill,
the Salvation Army blazing a trail past Ohio.
Should have set sail with the dead
Knights of Columbus not looking back—an icon
turned warning, that's useful. Instead I wrote
dead letters: *Leslie, give back the clock
with luminous hands. Send me
the bedspread.*

Sestina for Love Leaving

Morning roof. In shivering limbs the lilac
leaf miner goes about his work: sucks the thin
leaves dry. Where I compose a tree's
dead bones with apple cheeks against flat sky,
this larva in the news weaves lightly
towards the skeleton. A good day for both,

the story goes. In trees and bushes, both
remind me of the lying close in lilac-
scented leaves. Purple stole across the lightly
moving limbs and plumes of summer gone. Thin
aureoles of plum and violet wing, the sky
held down. This windy day becomes the trees.

You said, *No flickers in the browntone trees.*
None in your eyelids, closed on morning sun. Both
take daylight somewhere far away, the sky
inviting sleep. When silver mesh turns lilac
in night air, we watch three spinners weave thin
film like the miner's web. Turning lightly,

they interlace the sky these lightly
arched limbs mould. The cedar shakes and trees
send creaky tunes underground, vibrate thin
wires that carry borrowed light to both
poles. At intervals, the nodes turn blood lilac
where the vein strokes light. Subtly changing sky

nails a scaffold down at noon—dun sky
drawn back behind the hill it follows. Lightly
spoken lovers' words part air: *This lilac
drowns the yard in scent, turning all the trees
to skeletons against the pane.* When both
marrow and music reappear in thin

rituals of smoke, glass trees strike winter-thin
air. If vapor trails festoon the night sky

73

we bless our lifted bodies and dare both
planets to settle. Colonies of lightly
humming stars on grass. Conspiracy of trees
to net the space we opened, falling. Lilac

and parasitic blue, thin snow of lightly
drifting bloom, sky pours on reliquary trees.
The spines both hands define: remembered lilac.

New England Interlude

None of this seems real, seen from the east
and older. The red-eyed Guernsey bull,
his warning signal
turned on lunging cars. Trucks
stopped by the stooks of corn. This wilderness
is Thickly Settled
and the Berkshires' blue
surrounds my day.

           In Amherst, everything checked
in its fall: sacrificial stance of thistle,
flash of pumpkins in the field,
tomatoes stopped
on the withered vine. Here, tents
are made by caterpillars
or made of gauze and mean
shade-grown tobacco.

           Rococo time. The Rouault-red
of fall: sculptured mastiff
chained to the barn door,
alert for the smallest opening. Mill River,
low over the dam,
the sumac's plume still
red as the flag behind the final tee
at Cherry Hill.

           Into this flat sky,
western peaks lift. Their snowy desolations
call across my sleep.
And will I go back with the reddening
salmon, escape the long upstream
of traffic, my Nova rusted out,
to a town in full view
of the sea?

           What visionary company
follows the wale of water, crest and trough,

to hang on the seaward side
of Humbug Mountain?
A vertical drop, no breaker-
cut shelf for roadway, surf not dragging
shallow bottom, but slapping the face gently
where I ride the skiff of my body
into the seventh wave.

The Leopard

. . . all animals of a given species are sacred

My files bulge with letters from the dead:
the pale young man whose vision would
outlive me. The other, made
executor, commanding eye
trained on the dangerous words. He let them
die by dying first and early:

                     all that care,
law's complex instruments in hands that shook
themselves to prop the sense of being
in control. Now when the jungle slips from chains
to stalk my room,

                  the corporation sole
dismisses animal worship, waits
on the funeral. The ticker-tape is read:
in that parade, red tape
at feet and head and not a dry eye present
including mine. The caged
still dead

          weeping under weeping birch: blurred
world I saw at ten's
safari into mist on windows and their prospects—
the family lens. I watch
the live flush creep into the willow whips
turned pale chartreuse

             and call that challenger
forth. The schooled beast
leaps from the chest—with everything to lose—
jolted by the last weak charge
into a country more commodious than birth.

Boatsong for Karen

All autumn, re-reading your letters, my student
dead on the threshold, I am drawn to a ledge
so high that I do not know
whether I can turn back. I try not to look
down, not to cheapen your act by maudlin
reminders. There's a welt on my shoulder
where a torpid hornet implanted a sting. Each
morning I drowse in a hot
bath until blood keels round. The pulse I try
to ignore beats from occupied

                                  quarters on a lower
floor. It puts me to sleep, rides down with me, up—
moving and still. It is the floor
I get off on, the unmade
music I wake to. Accustomed to cold extremities,
I order my feet to grip
ground. Your word leaps from the page
no longer the tune of a hired crooner: *alone
loneliness, lonely*. A chainsaw loud as hornets
doles out the log I burn.

                          Sun teeters a while
on the sill, is carried off under blankets. I imagine
your voice, real as the winter king's call
to Jung's dreaming girl. She wakes to her own cold
fingers closed on flesh of her belly. She is not
afraid. I am always afraid, the import
clear every time: *that she felt no fear of congealed
life, did not augur well*. Warm blood
plunges to the level of the understatement: *At 26
she took her own life*.

                      I take up my life. It is still
heavy. Vertical feet in a downward procession
throng the angelic straits of my window. Eyes boarded
over, the sculptured head with the high

coiffure. No good to remember
the first coffin, a bassinet, a case for jewels.
I carry the bones carefully. *Momentum:* what keeps us
moving, the chute of mass and velocity
we are rushing down. *Gravity:* the apple of discord
swoops down like a kite,

                    forked tail—good and evil.
String slips through the fingers, sand
in ethereal tides washed
brokenly ashore. *Where the poem lives:* far off the main-
land among shooting stars and revolving
figures of earth. *Lacunae:* ravines too deep to ignore.
Something is missing—a pit, a depression, white
wings of a boat waiting to be filled.

Extended Outlook

November days, and the vague shape of a wing,
of a claw at the sill, at the drawn
shade of the bedroom,
signals the oncoming freeze. Setting
the scent-baited trap for the shadow mouse
back of the dark pine cabinet,
the tenant hears the cat downstairs
whining to be let in.

                    The tree is a violin bow
scraping the sound box of the house
all day. Close to the ribbed
breath, the scrolled end of wind under the eaves
turns back on the fine-tuned neck,
answers the shrill
jay in the caterwaul of blue
and falling light.

                  Trying to score this weather
for strings, no hurricane, but a planned
diminuendo, I pretend that the house is my own;
the cat, my pet. That Canada
wishes me well. That the blue shriek and the wail
are a cradlesong and the gulf
repeating this gale in my ear, is an old friend
or no friend of mine.

Subject Front View, Subject Rear View

Two color photos—house in the Treasure State—
the only one I've owned,
framed in homely captions by a certified
appraiser. Say it's a more-than-halfway
house, it's gone—my life
removed—to the Roman Catholic Bishop of Montana
and the corporation sole.

                        At night I double back
on the still life of those rooms.
In every grate, a live coal
tends its weight of sleeping thunder. Morning
light is a well in the middle
of the kitchen. Slowly, it fills and overflows,
reaches out to the hall   pantry   bedroom
where things define themselves: I am chair

bookcase   floor lamp   table   I am vanity.
See how the static
nightgown on its hook, electric hem tucked up,
charges the manner of its putting by.
Whether we go or stay, it is the same
grief. Whether we leave or are left, the radio
blares in the echoing room

                        so we won't come home
to the truth we are always coming home to. Shut out
from the life of its body, a hooded figure
crouches at the tight-wound feet. A white moth
flutters near, cut from the breath
it floated on. The obbligato cat all day,
coat thickening against the snow,

                        gives one more sign
by which to read the adversary shadow.
Again I am outside: flanked by mountain ash and cedar,

my house stands in the tense
present, its backyard plum and apple. Lamplight
gathers up its complicated life
in stages for the elevated window. My place
was in the cave of darkness

                                near the bottom stair.
"Pull down the blind," my mother would have said,
throwing a silhouette on the lowered shade.
I hear her admonition nightly as the cold curtain
rings down. Back for unfinished reels, I must
begin as if I would complete them. Never mind
the clearly imagined

                            wings of my house, there are
wheels on my luggage. Heroic figures
cloud the silver screen
and news of the ghostly world filters in.

Notes: Imaginary Ancestors

"GERARD MAJELLA": According to saintly legend the Redemptorist lay brother, Gerard Majella (1726–1755), was adept at the art of being in two places at once. Forbidden by superiors to work miracles without permission, he was walking one day past a building just as a laborer fell from the scaffolding. Gerard pointed his finger at the man in mid-air and said, "Stay there until I get permission!"

GILBERT OF SEMPRINGHAM": The "religious name" of Gilbert was given to the speaker rather than chosen by her. Little is known of the English saint aside from the details mentioned in the poem. Actually, both the men's and women's orders established by him continue to the present day. The first Holy Names Sisters in the United States to bear this name spent many years in the Oregon province of the congregation.

Biographical Note

MADELINE DEFREES directs the MFA Program in Creative Writing at the University of Massachusetts in Amherst. A native Oregonian, she taught for twelve years at the University of Montana and for short periods at the University of Washington, Seattle University and the University of Victoria. A member until 1973 of the Sisters of the Holy Names of Jesus and Mary, she published earlier prose and poems under the name of Sister Mary Gilbert. Her first teaching assignments were in schools and colleges of the Congregation throughout the Northwest, the longest at Holy Names College, Spokane, renamed Fort Wright College.

DeFrees has contributed short fiction to the *Iowa Review*, the *Virginia Quarterly Review* and other journals, as well as to *Best American Short Stories*.

Recipient of a Guggenheim Fellowship and a National Endowment for the Arts grant, she is spending the year on the Oregon Coast.

A Note on the Type

B E M B O is a revival of a roman cut by Francesco Griffo for the Venetian printer Aldus Manutius. It was first used in Cardinal Bembo's *De Aetna*, 1495, hence the name of the contemporary version.

The type for this book, 12 point, was set by Irish Setter in Portland, Oregon.